MW00364995

# HOW TO GET A
# JOB AT AMAZON
# & BIG TECH

## — INSIDER'S TIPS TO EXCEL IN YOUR
## BEHAVIORAL INTERVIEW

*100+ REAL INTERVIEW QUESTIONS AND MODEL RESPONSES FROM
AMAZON, MICROSOFT, GOOGLE & FACEBOOK*

**Max Magnus**

# INTRODUCTION

Interviewing with a massive tech firm like Amazon is a significantly different experience than interviewing with any other 'normal' company. *Believe me.* Despite the popular but incorrect belief, many tech companies do not adopt brainteasers or paradox questions. These are simply not good predictors of job success or performance. Tech companies also don't typically use traditional interviewing that focuses on resume information alone (i.e., company name, job title, job description, etc.). Amazon, Microsoft, Facebook and Google use the behavioral interviewing method. This is based on the idea that the best predictor of future performance is past performance.

I've worked at Amazon and Microsoft, and interviewed at Facebook and Google (the "Big Four"). I've also been a hiring manager and "bar raiser" at Amazon, and have been a hiring manager at Microsoft. These are my insights.

I aim to share my experience and provide you with an insider's perspective into the thinking behind the hiring process and equip you with the types of behavioral questions (over 120 in Chapter 5), and expected responses, actually used and adopted by the Big Four. I don't give you the answers – those need to come from your own experiences. I also don't intend to give you in-depth career guidance. I intend to give you the *mental model* within which to apply your experiences in answering the questions, and *what* interviewers are looking for in your answers. I also give some key tips on how you can prepare for an interview in Chapter 6.

Getting an interview (and, hopefully, an offer) from any of these four awesome companies is a big deal. They are the best technology companies in the world. I hope these insights help you to prepare so you feel more comfortable during what is a very intense, but rewarding, process. All the best for this next step ahead of you!

– Max

# CONTENTS

# 1. HIRING AND INTERVIEW PROCESS

The interview process is fairly similar for hiring across different roles in the Big Four. Interviewers use phone screenings, an onsite loop, then internally debrief. This is the typical process:

1. **Phase 1 – Getting recruited**: the company's in-house recruiter will reach out to you about the role. Use the recruiter as a resource for further information about the role, manager and other tips and tricks for landing the role.

2. **Phase 2 – First phone interview:** conducted by your peer from the team that you're interviewing for. This typically takes 30 mins.

3. **Phase 3 – Second phone interview:** conducted by a team member typically with more seniority than the last interviewer. This is where you may be asked to demonstrate your technical ability (either on the call, via a take home assessment, or both).

4. **Phase 4 – Onsite interviews:** ranges from three to seven interviews (60 minutes each) depending on your seniority level. This means you'll have to ensure your energy levels will meet the three to seven hours of interviewing.

5. **Phase 5 – The offer**: your hiring manager or recruiter will do the honors and reach out to you to confirm the company would like to make you an offer. Congratulations! Hang tight while the company sends you the job terms in an offer letter and employment contract. And remember, the first offer is just an initial one – if you're not happy with the terms always try to negotiate. Otherwise, sign away!

# Interview format

Here's an example format of a 60-minute interview:

- **Introduction** *(5 – 10 minutes)*: Introduce yourself (you can ask questions at the end).

- **Interview questions** *(40 minutes)*: Leadership principles and technical/functional skills.

- **Your questions** *(5 – 10 minutes)*: This is your chance to ask questions about the company, the team, and the interviewer's experience at the company.

From my experience, interviews with Amazon, Microsoft, Google and Facebook are similar in their rigor. I found my Amazon interview to be the hardest, but I found the other interview experiences not too dissimilar in intensity with only slight variances. My Microsoft interview was not as difficult as either Amazon, Google or Facebook, but it was not easy by any means.

Here are the key differences:

- Amazon's interview process is incredibly rigorous. The loop is tech heavy, and also includes behavioral interview questions that intend to probe your knowledge and experience deeply. There is always an internal debrief with all data points (i.e., your response content and how you responded) considered. The "bar raiser" and hiring manager attend to ensure the bar is met and overall hiring guidelines are followed. This includes ensuring the "hiring bar" concept is applied. A hire is never made unless the candidate "raises the bar" overall. Amazon's hiring **bar** is never lowered. (These concepts are explained further in the next section.)

- Microsoft has a similar structure but the hiring decision at Microsoft is made by the "As-App" (As Appropriate).

- Facebook and Google interviews are similar, but normally take less time. From my experience, and speaking with many other candidates, I found

4

Google's hiring bar to be close to Amazon's in terms of technical intensity. The same for Facebook, minus the in depth behavioral interviewing.

# 2. AMAZON'S "BAR RAISER" AND MICROSOFT'S "AS-APP"

Amazon uses the concept of "bar raisers (BRs)." BRs are objective third parties (i.e., Amazon employees outside the organization and team for which your interviewing) who attend every interview loop. The role of BRs is to help make the best long-term hiring decisions for the company. Just like all other interviewers in the loop, the BR interviews the candidate, writes feedback, and casts their hiring vote during the internal debrief. In addition to these tasks, the BR also leads the debrief. All interviewers have a say in the hiring decision but, ultimately, the BR and hiring manager must both agree to hire a candidate before an offer can be made.

At Microsoft, the hiring decision is made by the "As-App" (As Appropriate). This is normally, but not always, your last interview. And, while overall data points are considered, As-Apps frequently veto or hire independently of the overall data, and make the hiring decision solely based on their own impressions. There is also not always a debrief, however, this is the exception not the rule. Normally, the hiring manager speaks with the As-App and they decide together. This is a significant difference to the Amazon process and is neither right, wrong or indifferent – it is just the Microsoft process, and it works well for Microsoft.

# *Amazon Hiring Bar*

The Amazon hiring bar has two criteria - both must be met in order to hire a candidate:

1. **Your performance and results**: First, is this person better than 50% of the people currently performing in this role at Amazon?
    a. You'll be evaluated based on your past **performance and results** from your experience and background.
    b. The 50% is an internal benchmark for Amazon employees, in the same job type and at the same level, and not externally compared to other candidates.
    c. Amazon evaluates each candidate against the Amazon hiring bar; not against each other.
2. **How you'll contribute:** Second, does this candidate have upside growth potential to offer long-term impact at Amazon?
    a. You'll be assessed on whether you can excel in the Amazon environment, over time, by focusing on the Amazon Leadership Principles (how you contribute).
    b. In addition to you past performance, you'll be evaluated for potential growth. This tests whether can you continue to expand your contribution and role.

A hire or no-hire decision is substantiated with specific evidence to support why Amazon is, or is not, hiring this candidate. The debrief discussion is focused on one candidate against the hiring bar for that role or level.

If there are multiple candidates for a role, each candidate is assessed against the hiring bar for the role. When there is more than one candidate who raises the bar (and the BR agrees), the hiring manager can make the final decision about who to hire into that specific role. Only candidates who raise the bar are offered positions at Amazon.

# 3. HOW YOUR PERFORMANCE IS ASSESSED

To assess your *performance*, tech companies typically assign functional or technical competencies to interviewers. In Amazon, the assigned competencies are a combination of Amazon's "Leadership Principles", and functional and technical skills. The hiring manager assigns up to two competencies to each interviewer. Interviewers use these to assess each candidate and report back their feedback during the internal debrief.

At every stage of the hiring process – resume review, phone screens, onsite interviews, written feedback and the debrief – the interviewer's primary role is to assess a candidate's performance, competencies, and results against the relevant criteria (e.g., the Amazon hiring bar) for the appropriate role and level.

Assessment focuses on performance (hard skills), competencies (soft skills), and results (impact). These are key differentiators that provide them with evidence and data points to substantiate and support a hiring decision.

The following is the type of exemplary assessment criterion used:

| To assess... | Drill down on... | Interview will ask ... |
|---|---|---|
| Performance | Functional expertise | What is this candidate great at? |
| Competencies | Leadership principles | Does this candidate demonstrate the company's values? |

| Results | Measures of accomplishment | What can this candidate contribute? How will they impact the team and company? |
|---|---|---|

# 4. BEHAVIORAL INTERVIEWING WITH 'STAR'

Amazon, Microsoft, Facebook and Google use the *behavioral interviewing* method. This is based on the idea that the best predictor of future performance is past performance.

Behavioral interviewing focuses on asking questions to understand how a candidate behaved in past situations as a way to predict future behavior in similar situations. The **STAR** (situation, task, action, result) method is used to gather all the relevant information about specific capabilities a role requires.

Interviewers at Amazon, Microsoft, Facebook and Google ask behavioral questions, and probe and challenge using the STAR method. Behavioral questions are open-ended and aim to generate specific examples from candidates. This is to help the interviewer evaluate performance and long-term impact at the same time.

Behavioral Question Sample: *Give me an example of a project you're working on that could have significantly impact on the business or customer.*

Refer to the Behavioral Interview Question Bank. This is a valuable resource to use for behavioral interviews (see Chapter 5).

## *Examples of behavioral interviewing with STAR*

Interviewers use behavioral questions and probe with STAR to get the full story. Here are some examples.

**SITUATION/TASK – Describe the situation/task you faced and the context of the example.**

Answer the questions with: **where** did this occur, **when** did it happen, **why** is it important?

**Probing Questions:**
- Why is this important? What was the goal?
- What was the initial scope of the project? What were the challenges?
- What were the risks and potential consequences if nothing happened?

**Challenge Questions:**
- Why did you choose this example to illustrate xyz accomplishment?
- What other examples can you think of that demonstrate xyz?
- Could you come up with an example that is more recent?

**ACTION – What actions did you take?**

Answer the questions with: **what** did you personally own, **how** did you do it, **who** else was involved?

**Probing Questions:**
- Deep probe into functional expertise and/or assigned core competency.
- Were you the key driver or project owner?
- What was your biggest contribution? What unique value did you bring?
- What were the most significant obstacles you faced? How did you overcome them?

**Challenge Questions:**
- What did you specifically do versus the team?
- How did you set priorities to deal with xyz problem or get manager buy-in?
- What decisions did you challenge? Why? How did you influence the right outcome?

**RESULTS – How did you measure success for this project? What results did you achieve?**
- Cost savings, revenue generation.
- Quantify to understand volume, size, scale.
- Percentage change, year over year improvements.
- Time to market, implementation time, time savings.
- Impact on the customer, the team.
- Quality improvements.

**Probing Questions:**
- Why did you choose to focus on these results? What other results

were important?

- You mentioned revenue, what percentage change is that year over year?
- What trade-offs did you have to make to achieve this? (quality, cost, time)
- I'm concerned about the time it took, the volume, the customer impact, tell me more.

**Challenge Questions:**

- What were the lessons learned? What would you have done differently?
- How would you improve the process or result today?
- How would you implement this at the Company?
- How did these results compare to your actual goals? (refer back to the goal stated in situation)

# 5. BEHAVIOURAL INTERVIEW QUESTION BANK

The following is a series of questions and model responses taken from actual interviews from Amazon, Microsoft, Facebook and Google.

## *DEMONSTRATE HIGH JUDGEMENT*

Example Behavioral Interview Questions

1. Tell me about a decision for which data and analysis weren't sufficient to provide the right course and you had to rely on your judgment and instincts. Give me two to three examples. They don't have to be big strategic decisions - could be big or small.

2. Tell me about a time you made a difficult decision and how you knew it was the right solution (probe on how they evaluated the options, if thy received input, what data they reviewed, etc.)

3. Give me an example of when you have to make an important decision in the absence of good data because there just wasn't any. What was the situation and how did you arrive at your decision? Did the decision turn out to be the correct one? Why or why not?

4. Tell me about a time when your view on something important was significantly changed by someone that came from a different perspective? What was your reaction? What made you change your mind?

5. Tell me about a time where you sought out perspectives other than your own to make a product/service/project better

6. Tell me about a time when you made a bad decision and the learning from the experience enabled you to make a good decision later. What d id you learn that you were able to apply?

7. Tell me about a time when you have been faced with a challenge where the best way forward or strategy to adopt was not "clear cut" (i.e. there were a number of possible solutions). How did you decide the best way forward?

8. Tell me about an error in judgment you made in the last yea r or two, what it was and the impact of it.

9. Tell me about a business model decision or key technology decision or other important strategic decision you had to make for which there was not enough data or benchmarks. I n the absence of all the data, what guided your choice and how did you make the call? (follow- up with the alternatives considered and how/why they were ruled out in favor of the path taken, what was the risk mitigation strategy? Outcome? Ask for another example and potentially a third until you are sure this is a pattern and not a one off). (Manager)

10. What are the top strategic issues you 've had to face in your current role? What decisions did you end up making? (Manager)

| Your answer should include whether you: | |
| --- | --- |
| **As a people manager do you...** | **As an individual contributor do you...** |
| • Use sound business judgment to make the right decision quickly and achieve results, even in the absence of complete data? <br> • Question whether decisions are being made in the Company's and customer's best interest and change course when they are not? | |
| • Actively seek out the best solution, recognizing that great ideas often come from others? | • Recognize that your idea may not be as good as someone else's and get on board with the best idea? |

# DEMONSTRATE YOU'RE ACTION-ORIENTATED

Example Behavioral Interview Questions

1. Give me an example of a calculated risk that you have taken where speed was critical. What was the situation and how did you handle it? What steps did you take to mitigate the risk? What was the outcome?
2. Describe a situation where you made an important business decision without consulting your manager. What was the situation and how did it turn out?
3. Tell me about a time when you had to analyze facts quickly, define key issues, and respond immediately to a situation. What was the outcome?
4. Tell me about a time when you have worked against tight deadlines and didn't have the time to consider all options before making a decision. How much time d id you have? What approach did you take?
5. Give an example of when you had to make an important decision and had to decide between moving forward or gathering more information. What d id you do? What information is necessary for you to have before acting?
6. Tell me about a time where you felt your team was not moving to action quickly enough. What did you do? (Manager)
7. Tell me about a time when you were able to remove a serious road block/barrier preventing your team from making progress? How were you able to remove the barrier? What was the outcome? (Manager)

| Your answer should include whether: | |
|---|---|
| **As a people manager do you...** | **As an individual contributor do you...** |
| • Makes sound, timely decisions and remove barriers for direct reports? <br> • Quickly identify how work should be done and communicated to team? <br> • Make timely, sound decisions for the business even when all info you want to have isn't available? <br> • Empower your employees or become a bottleneck? <br> • Remove barriers to help your team act on new ideas immediately? | • Quickly identify if you need more info before taking action request that info and move forward? <br> • Be ready, willing and able to roll up sleeves and assist with customer facing tasks when needed? <br> • Ask for help when needed in a timely manner? <br> • Respond promptly to requests for information? <br> • Follow up and deliver as promised? <br> • Make sure you create an "action item list" (identify owner and target dates)? |

# DEMONSTRATE CUSTOMER FOCUS

Example Behavioral Interview Questions

1. Give me an example of a time you used customer feedback to drive improvement or in novation. What was the situation and what action did you take?

2. Give me an example of your most difficult customer interaction and how you worked through it. What was the outcome?

3. Tell me about a time a customer wanted one thing, but you felt they needed something else. How did you approach the situation, what were your actions and what was the end result?

4. Tell me about a time when you went above and beyond the call of duty for a customer. Why did you take the action you did? What was the outcome?

5. Most of us at one time or another have felt frustrated or impatient when dealing with customers. Can you tell us about a time when you felt this way and how you dealt with it? When do you think it's appropriate to push back or say no to an unreasonable customer request?

6. Can you give me an example of when you've been able to see around the corner to meet a customer need or delight a customer with a solution or product they didn't yet know they needed/wanted?

7. To try to meet the high expectations of our customers, we sometimes promise more than we can deliver. Tell me about a time when you overcommitted yourself or your company. How did you resolve the issue?

8. Tell me about a time when you had to balance the needs of the customer vs. the needs of the business. How did you manage this situation?

9. In your opinion, what is the most effective way to evaluate the quality of your product or service to your internal /external customer? Give an example of a time when you used these measures to make a decision. (Manager)

10. What changes have you implemented in your current department to meet the needs of your customers? What has been the result? (Manager)

## Your answer should include whether you:

- Know your customer's needs and wants?
- Anticipate your customer's needs?
- Honestly pursue customer feedback, not just solicit for compliments?
- "WOW" your customers?
- Know what would be better than what your customer is even imagining?
- Ask, "Is what I'm working on helping my customer?"
- Remove non-value steps?
- Listen for what your customer wants, before/instead of telling them what they need?

# DEMONSTRATE ABILITY TO DELIVERY RESULTS

Example Behavioral Interview Questions

1. Tell me about a time you (and your tea m if Manager) were driving toward a goa l and were more than half way to the objective when you realized it may not be the best or right goal or may have unintended consequences. What was the situation and what did you do? [Testing for achieving the right result versus driving goal for sake of goal achievement. May want follow up questions regarding to determine if the person was willing to take hit on goal attainment to achieve the right result and test long term versus short term thinking.]

2. Tell me about a goal that you set that took a long time to achieve or that you are still working towards. How do you keep focused on the goal given the other priorities you have?

3. Tell me about a time where you not only met a goal but considerably exceeded expectations. How were you able to do it? What challenges d id you have to overcome?

4. Give me an example of a time when you were able to deliver an important project under a tight dead line. What sacrifices did you have to make to meet the deadline? How did they impact the final deliverables?

5. Tell me about a time you had significant, unanticipated obstacles to overcome in achieving a key goal. Were you eventually successful?

6. How do you ensure you are focusing on the right deliverables when you have several com petting priorities? Tell me about a time when you did not effectively manage your projects and something fell through the cracks. (Manager)

7. What's your secret to success in setting stretch goa ls for your tea m that are challenging, yet achievable? Tell me about a time you didn't hit the right balance. How did you adjust? (Manager)

8. Give an example of a mission or goa l you didn't thin k was achievable. What was it and how did you help your team try to achieve it? Were you successful in the end? (Manager)

| Your answer should include whether: | |
|---|---|
| **As a people manager do you...** | **As an individual contributor do you...** |
| • Continually reinforce to yourself and the team who the customer is in order to execute and deliver the right results? | |
| • Set and communicate smart team goals, | • Focus on the most important |

| | |
|---|---|
| expectations and priorities; help employees stay focused, yet nimble and adaptable to moving targets or when projects aren't progressing in order to get things done?<br><br>• Help others remove barriers/road blocks towards meeting team goa ls?<br><br>• Recognize and celebrate successes, while keeping the team focused on delivering the right results? | tasks, while adapting as needed to achieve results?<br><br>• Persevere through setbacks and overcome obstacles to deliver outstanding results? |

# ABILITY TO THINK DEEPLY

Example Behavioral Interview Questions

1. Tell me about a time you were trying to understand a problem on your team and you had to go down several layers to figure it out. Who did you talk with and what information proved most valuable? How did you use that information to help solve the problem?
2. Tell me about a problem you had to solve that required in-depth thought and analysis? How did you know you were focusing on the right things?
3. Tell me about a time when you linked two or more problems together and identified an underlying issue? Were you able to find a solution?
4. Walk me through a big problem or issue in your organization that you helped to solve. How did you become aware of it? What information d id you gather, what information was missing and how did you fill the gaps?
   Did you do a post mortem analysis and if you did what did you learn?
5. Can you tell me about a specific metric you have used to identify a need for a change in your department? Did you create the metric or was it already available? How did this and other information influence the change?
6. Give me a situation in which it took you asking why five times to get to the root cause.
7. As a manager, how do you stay connected to the details while focusing on the strategic, bigger picture issues? Tell me about a time when you were too far removed from a project one of your employees was working on    and you ended up missing a goal (Manager)

| Your answer should include whether: | |
|---|---|
| **As a people manager do you...** | **As an individual contributor do you...** |
| • Not pass the buck on unwanted tasks, demonstrate hustle and a 'do what it takes' attitude to get things done, even if that means being hands-on? | |
| • Stay closely connected to the details of projects/business, knowing when to get involved without micromanaging? <br> • Frequently "audit" by drilling down into projects/business, questioning and providing feedback, quickly assessing progress and risk, and hold employees accountable for results? <br> • Drill down on fuzzy information, refusing to accept generalizations or light-weight responses? | • Have a firm grasp of the details of your work in order to deeply discuss it? <br> • Frequently "audit" your work by checking accuracy, facts and assumptions? |

# DEMONSTRATE LADERSHIP AND TEAM BEHAVIOR

Example Behavioral Interview Questions

1. Describe a time when you significantly contributed to improving morale and productivity on your team. What were the underlying problems and their causes? How did you prevent them from negatively impacting the team in the future?

2. What three things you are you working on to improve your overall effectiveness?

3. Give an example of a tough or critical piece of feedback you received. What was it and what d id you do about it?

4. Give me an example of an idea you had that was strongly opposed. Why was there so much resistance? How did you handle the negative feedback?

5. Give me an example of a significant professional failure. What led you to making the wrong decision? What did you learn from this situation?

6. Give an example of a time where you were not able to meet a commitment to a tea m member. What was the commitment and what prevented you from meeting it? What was the outcome and what d id you learn from it?

7. Building trust can be difficult to achieve at times. Tell me about how you have effectively built trusting working relationships with others on your team.

8. Describe a time when you needed the cooperation of a peer who was resistant. What d id you do? What was the outcome?

9. Tell me about a piece of direct feedback you recently gave to a colleague. How did s/he respond? How do you like to receive feedback from others?

10. Tell me about a time you had to communicate a big change in direction for which you anticipated people would have a lot of concerns. How did you handle questions and/or resistance? Were you able to get people comfortable with the change?

11. Tell me about a time your team's goals were out of alignment with another tea m on which you relied to attain a key resource. How did you work with the other team? Were you able to achieve your goals? (Manager)

12. Tell me about a time you uncovered a significant problem in your team. What was it and how did you communicate it to your manager and to your peers or other stakeholders? (Manager)

| Your answer should include whether: | |
|---|---|
| **As a people manager do you...** | **As an individual contributor do** |

| | you... |
|---|---|
| • Earn the trust and respect of the team and build positive working relationships by consistently making good decisions, keeping commitments, treating others and their ideas with respect, and adhering to high ethical standards? | |
| • Provide an environment where team members have room to take smart risks and learn from mistakes while not losing sight of their accountability for results?<br>• Listen, communicate and delegate to help employees get the right things done? | • Do what you say you will do or appropriately reset expectations?<br>• Honor commitments made to other teams even if your own goals are in jeopardy? |

# DEMONSTRATE SELF-SUFFICIENCY AND RESOURCEFULNESS

Example Behavioral Interview Questions

1. Give me an example of how you have helped save costs or eliminate waste within your operation.
2. Tell me about a time when you had to make tradeoffs between quality and cost. How did you weigh the options? What was the result?
3. Tell me about a time you had to get something done with half or two thirds of the resources you thought you'd need for the project or initiative.
4. Tell me about a time when you generated a creative solution to a problem or project without requiring additional resources. What was the problem? What was the solution and how did you come up with it?
5. Tell me about a time you didn't have enough resources to do something you felt was important but found a creative way to get it done anyway. What drove you to seek out creative solutions?
6. Give an example of a time you requested additional fund in g/budget to complete a project. Why was it needed? Did you try to figure out another approach? Did you get the additional resources? Why or why not?
7. Give an example of a time when you challenged your team to come up with more efficient solution or process. What drove the request? How did you help? (Manager)
8. How do you determine when to award or ask for additional resources? What criteria do you use for making the call? (Manager)
9. Tell me how you have created organization (or customer) value through either increased revenue stream or lowering the cost structure. (Manager)

| Your answer should include whether: | |
| --- | --- |
| **As a people manager do you...** | **As an individual contributor do you...** |
| • Ask, "Does this spend make a positive impact for the customer? | |
| • Role model behaviors for team by not exhibiting 'hierarchical" behavior like ta king a larger office, expensing lunches, being extravagant?<br>• Being transparent with team about costs –creating a general awareness that things cost money?<br>• Understand the difference between frugal and cheap? | • Creatively spend money and share your resources?<br>• Seek out "no-cost" alternatives prior to spending? |

# DEMONSTRATE ABILITY TO DISAGREE AND COMMIT

Example Behavioral Interview Questions

1. Tell me about a time that you strongly disagreed with your manager on something you deemed to be very important to the business. What was it about and how did you handle it?
2. Give me an example of when you took an unpopular stance in a meeting with peers and your leader and you were the outlier. What was it, why did you feel strongly about it, and what did you do?
3. When do you decide to go along with the group decision even if you disagree? Give me an example of a time you chose to acquiesce to the group even when you disagreed. Would you make the same decision now?
4. Describe a time where you felt really strongly about something but ultimately lost the argument. How hard did you press the issue? What was your approach after you lost the argument?
5. Give an example when you submitted a good idea to your manager and he/she did not take action on it? How did you handle it? What was the end outcome?
6. Tell me about a time the business gained something because you persisted for a length of time. Why were you so determined? How did it turn out?
7. Provide an example of a time when you have had to make a difficult decision under pressure and then defend and justify it. Was it the right decision?
8. Give an example of when you had to support a business initiative with which you didn't necessarily agree. How did you handle it? (Manager)
9. Tell me about a time when you pushed back against a decision that negatively impacted your team. What was the issue and how did it turn out? (Manager)

| Your answer should include whether: | |
|---|---|
| **As a people manager do you...** | **As an individual contributor do you...** |
| • Question rigorously, challenge assumptions and escalate issues up and across the "food chain" when you're not satisfied, even if unpopular? | |
| • Stand up for what you believe is in the best interest of the company and our customers? | |
| • Openly demonstrate your support and commitment to<br>• decisions that have been made, even though you may not have originally agreed? Refrain from being transparent with these types of decisions in the best interests of your employees? | • Get on board with decisions that have been made, even though you may not have originally agreed? |

# DEMONSTRATE HIGH STANDARDS

Example Behavioral Interview Questions

1. Tell me about a time when you have been unsatisfied with the status quo. What did you do to change it? Were you successful?
2. Tell me about a time you wouldn't compromise on achieving a great outcome when others felt something was good enough. What was the situation?
3. What measures have you personally put in place to ensure performance improvement targets and standards are achieved?
4. Describe the most significant, continuous improvement project that you have led. What was the catalyst to this change and how did you go about it?
5. Give me an example of a goal you've had where you wish you had done better. What was the goal and how could you have improved on it?
6. Tell me about a time when you have worked to improve the quality of a product /service/solution that was already getting good customer feedback? Why did you think it needed continued improvement?
7. Give an example where you refused to compromise your standards around quality/customer service, etc. Why did you feel so strongly about the situation? What were the consequences? The result?
8. How do you seek out feedback on your team's performance? Give a specific example of how you used feedback you received on your team to drive improvement. (Manager)
9. Can you tell me about a time when a team member was not being as productive as you needed? What was the situation? What did you do? What was the result? (Manager)
10. Describe the process you go through to set specific targets to improve critical areas of your work/team. Please refer to a specific example. (Manager)

| Your answer should include whether: | |
|---|---|
| **As a people manager do you...** | **As an individual contributor do you...** |
| • Raise the quality bar by demanding that your team delivers high quality products, services and solutions? | • Ensure the quality bar remains high by delivering high quality work, and demanding it of others' work? |
| • Teach and coach employees about setting their own high standards and exceeding customer expectations? | • Continually self-critique your work to make sure the quality is the best it can be? |
| • Provide feedback to employees when work is of high quality and coach to continually improve work? | • Accept and seek out coaching and feedback from your manager and others about improving the quality of your work? |

# DEMONSTRATE AN ABILITY TO INNOVATE

Example Behavioral Interview Questions

1. Tell me about the most innovative thing you've done and why you thought it was innovative (can also probe with: That sounds more evolutionary than revolutionary -tell me about something you've done you feel was truly revolutionary? Ask for one or two additional examples to see if it's a one off or pattern.)

2. People often say the simplest solution is the best. Tell me about a particular complex problem you solved with a simple solution.

3. Tell me about a time you were able to make something significantly simpler for customers. What drove you to implement this change?

4. Describe a challenging problem or situation in which the usual approach was not going to work. Why were you unable to take the usual approach? What alternative approach did you take? Was it successful?

5. Give an example of a creative idea you had that proved really difficult to implement. What was the idea and what made it difficult to implement? Was it successful?

6. Tell me about an out-of-the-box idea you had or decision you made that had a big impact on your business.

7. Give me an example of how you have changed the direction or view of a specific function/department and helped them embrace a new way of thin king? Why was a change needed?

8. How do you draw new thinking and innovation out of your team? Give an example of how your approach led to a specific innovation. (Manager)

9. Tell me about a time when you have enabled your team/ a tea m member to implement a significant change or improvement. (Manager)

| Your answer should include whether: | |
|---|---|
| **As a people manager do you...** | **As an individual contributor do you...** |
| • Simplify and always encourage others to in novate and change inefficient or unnecessarily complex processes? | |
| • Use new ideas and methods to do you r job better and enhance the customer experience? | |
| • Create an environment that encourages breakthrough thinking that is simple? <br> • Encourage in novation and invention for the right reasons, helping others not to un necessarily reinvent the wheel? | • Think up and implement great ideas and simple <br> • Solutions? <br> • Know when not to reinvent the wheel? |

# DEMONSTRATE ABILITY TO LEARN AND CURIOSITY

Example Behavioral Interview Questions

1. What is the coolest thing you have learned on your own that has helped you better perform your job?
2. Tell me about a time when you realized you needed to have a deeper level of subject matter expertise to do your job well?
3. When we enter into a new role or problem space, it is common to come in and see things with a fresh perspective. Tell me about a time when you realized that you might have lost that fresh perspective? What ended up happening?
4. Tell me of a time when you took on work outside of your comfort area and found it rewarding?
5. Tell me about a time when you didn't know what to do next or how to solve a challenging problem?
6. Example of a time when you pushed the existing boundaries beyond what was normal and expected for your space and you explored new territory?
7. How have you kept up to date with market and competitor trends, and used that information to improve your company's products/services?
8. Give me an example of a time when you challenged the notion that something had to be done a certain way because it had always been done that way?
9. What are you working on to improve your overall effectiveness at work?
10. Tell me about a time when you challenged your team to push the envelope and go beyond existing standards and expectations. (Manager)
11. Give a specific example of where you realized your team had not been as effective as it could have. What feedback mechanisms do you use? (Manager)
12. Example when someone on your team challenged you to think differently about a problem? What was the situation, how did you respond? (Manager)
13. Example where your team was unable to achieve a goal or milestone but the information gathered during the project enabled future success. (Manager)
14. Tel l me about a time when a member of your team contributed significantly to a project outside the scope of their role. What motivated you to encourage their participation? (Manager)

| Your answer should include whether: | |
| --- | --- |
| **As a people manager do you...** | **As an individual contributor do you...** |
| • Give your team members time to explore and learn?<br>• Encourage your team members to take risks and support them in doing so?<br>• Focus on how you arrived at the results rather than the results themselves?<br>• Encourage rotations to provide new opportunities for your team members to learn new skills? | • Take time to read, watch a tech talk, or actively mentor someone else?<br>• Ask you r peers, manager, and customers for feedback on your performance?<br>• Pick up work outside your area of expertise to stretch and grow?<br>• Take time to understand your systems end to end?<br>• Actively seek out advice from others? |

# DEMONSTRATE OWNERSHIP

Example Behavioral Interview Questions

1. Tell me about a time when you took on something significant outside your area of responsibility. Why was it important? What was the outcome?
2. Give me an example of a time when you didn't think you were going to meet the commitments you promised. How did you identify the risk and communicate it to stakeholders? What was the outcome?
3. Tell me about a time you made a hard decision to sacrifice short term gain for a longer-term goal.
4. Give an example of when you saw a peer struggling and decided to step in and help. What was the situation and what actions did you take? What was the outcome?
5. What steps do you take to ensure projects you complete get transitioned effectively to new owners? Give an example where you elected to re-engage on a project that you had already transitioned to someone else. What was the situation and why did you feel it was important to re-engage?
6. How do you ensure your tea m stays connected to the company vision and the bigger picture? Give an example of when you felt a tea m or individual goal was in conflict with the company vision. What did you do? (Manager)
7. Tell me about an initiative you undertook because you saw that it could benefit the whole company or your customers, but wasn't within any group's individual responsibility so nothing was being done. (Manager)

| Your answer should include whether: | |
|---|---|
| **As a people manager do you...** | **As an individual contributor do you...** |
| • Create a vision for your team that aligns with the customer experience? <br> • Foster an environment of autonomy where an employee prioritizes and make decisions? <br> • Think about the impact of your decisions on other teams, sites and the customer over time? <br> • Coach and mentor your team to understand the big picture, how their role supports the overall objectives of the company, and how it ties to others? | • Ask questions? <br> • Consider future outcomes (scalable, long-term value, etc.)? <br> • Give feedback -coach and develop others (peers, associates, manager)? <br> • Speak up in meetings -question, challenge respectfully? <br> • Understand your role and relationship with other roles? <br> • Understand the impact of your work on others? <br> • Partner with peers across the network? |

# DEMONSTRATE BIG-THINKING

Example Behavioral Interview Questions

1. Give me an example of a radical approach to a problem you proposed. What was the problem and why did you feel it required a completely different way of thinking about it? Was your approach successful?

2. How do you drive adoption for your vision/ideas? How do you know how well your idea or vision has been adopted by other teams or partners? Give a specific example highlighting one of your ideas.

3. Tell me about time you were working on an initiative or goal and saw an opportunity to do something much bigger than the initial focus.

4. Tell me about a time you looked at a key process that was working well and questioned whether it was still the right one? What assumptions were you questioning and why? Did you end up ma king a change to the process?

5. Tell me about a time you took a big risk - what was the risk, how did you decide to do it and what was the outcome?

6. Now Tell me about a time you took a big risk and it failed. What did you learn? What would you do differently?

7. Tell me about a time you came up with the vision for a (team, product, strategic initiative) when there wasn't a guiding vision. What was it? How did you gain buy-in and drive execution? (Manager)

8. Tell me about encouraging or enabling a member of your team to take big risk. How did you balance the risk to the business with possible positive outcome for the organization and opportunity for learning for your direct report? (Manager)

9. Tell me about time you had to develop a product/business model from scratch or when you dramatically changed one in a turnaround situation. (Manager)

| Your answer should include whether: | |
| --- | --- |
| **As a people manager do you...** | **As an individual contributor do you...** |
| • Take a radical approach and risks when necessary, always questioning traditional assumptions in pursuit of the biggest and best idea? | |

| | |
|---|---|
| • Create a gutsy mission that employees can be inspired by and get behind; provide direction for how to get there and explain how everything fits into the long -term plan?<br>• Continually communicate the big picture and mission to the team in a manner that gets employees excited (as a result, employees want to get out of bed and come to work each day)?<br>• Actively explore new ideas from team members, encouraging risk taking when appropriate? | • Translate broader mission into big, hairy ideas and tactics in your own work?<br>• Ask questions to get a sense of direction and confirm how work fits into the short- and long term picture?<br>• Hungrily accept the challenge to create the best idea/solution and take risks? |

# 6. HOW CAN YOU PREPARE FOR AN INTERVIEW?

1. **Do your homework**. You want to study the job description and company you'll be interviewing with to help you prepare for a behavioral-based interview. If you can, find out some info about the last or current incumbent of the position and the types of employees the organization hires. This will help you come up with a list of competencies, attributes, and skills, which is discussed in the next paragraph.

2. **Come up with a list of competencies, attributes, and skills**. Behavioral interview questions will give you the chance to showcase your talent, ability, and results. To prepare, you'll want to think about the type of competencies the company is looking for. Most companies will look for similar competencies, attributes, and skills, such as communication, team player, ability to focus, efficiency, timeliness, flexibility, attention to detail, management and leadership material, creativity, goal orientation and responsibility. Take a moment to rank the list you come up with in relation to the position for which you are applying. In Amazon, this will link to the Leadership Principles.

3. **Create a list of your past experiences**. Make a list of your past experiences and successes that highlight the list of competencies, skills, and attributes you come up with, as noted in the point above. Come up with good antidotes and stories, as we all love a good story. With that said, you want to keep your answers focused and to-the-point.

4. **Focus on the good and the not-so-good.** Don't forget to come up with some examples or scenarios that were challenging, yet you pulled through successfully. Such examples showcase your problem-solving skills and ability to handle challenges professionally. You might also be asked how you might handle such situations differently, so be prepared to discuss your areas for improvement, as well.

5. **Use the STAR method.** When coming up with examples, write down the Situation or Task you had to resolve, the Action(s) you took, and the Results of the situation. Use specifics, such as people, places, scale, and scope, and quantify as much as possible. Provide details that can be verified by references in case the employers decide to check.

6. **Look at past performance documents and appraisals.** To prepare for future job interviews, look back at past performance appraisals and notes to help you identify achievements and situations that will help you come up with examples for a behavioral interview.

7. **Begin taking notes now.** If you're not currently working, then this might not apply to you; but could still be good to take note of for the future. Document your successes, achievements and so on, while you're working to help you come up with stories and examples for behavioral interviews in the future. This will also help you when it comes to completing performance appraisals if you're required to do so.

# ABOUT THE AUTHOR

Max Magnus is an author, entrepreneur, and speaker based in Seattle, USA. Max has written a number of instructional and self-development guides, with a focus on tools developed from cognitive behavior therapy. Max's goal is to help other people live life a little fuller.

Made in the USA
Las Vegas, NV
13 August 2021

28128035R00020